It'll All Work Out

Bay Alexander

Library of Congress Cataloging-in-Publication Data

Alexander Bay

It'll All Work Out -- 1st Ed.

p. cm.

ISBN: 9798366994729

Contents

Prologue

♥

T he family story is that as a very young child I would sit on my grandfathers lap and we'd baby chat. I wasn't able to say the word "baby," so I called myself Bay. I've been Bay ever since.

As the last of four siblings I was the cute, funny one. No one ever thought I had anything interesting or important to say. I've been finding ways to be heard ever since. In the beginning my only way of engaging was to launch a full on argument, ending it with "Well anyway Bay!"

This book is a lifetime of thoughts waiting to be shared. It evolved over many years. At first I was keeping a diary. In time I had started to keep journals adding my emotions, and opinions, keeping track of things I love and feelings that touched my heart and imagination. When I started to write it was just for the pleasure of losing myself in the thoughtful, inspirational process of writing. On a whim I decided to take an on-line writing class. I loved it. There were deadlines, helpful, critical, information and heartwarming encouragement. Then my life changed dramatically. My writing was set aside.

Forty years later I moved to Santa Barbara. Suddenly l had lots of time . . . and then endless time, as COVID changed everything. For a long time, we were to shelter in place. It's been a time to look back, revisiting all I have written. Finally, I began to think of putting it all together in a book about things and qualities I believe are timeless: connections, caring, whimsy, growing, laughing, learning, and, most of all, about Love.

I encourage readers to browse. Different pieces may be meaningful at different times. After all, for most of us, our lives are not one long planned story. It 's an olio, an accumulation of bits and pieces that become our personal story.

Days

One day flies by in a flow of
purpose.
The next day takes forever to
find its way.
Good days, bad days, who
am I to judge them?

I'm thankful for
them all. Laughter
and sadness
dance together
blending memories
that last forever.
We are what our
days are, the world
plows on with a
purpose of its own, while our

1

choices weave themselves
into the fabric of our days.
Heart and head lead us
forward
With unplanned creativity
as we blossom into newness.
Our days fill with precious
memories that will last
forever.
Time goes by like a long
movie. As scenes flash by I
wonder
Haven't I seen this movie
before? Newness now is
looking back.
What have I done? What
have I learned? What is
worth leaving
behind? Stories can be told
and wisdom shared, yet
nothing is really
new. Our memories are
sheltering in place, a wealth
of joyful treasures.

Living Our Lives

♥

Busy Is Good

Mrs. Stedman was a busy woman. Every day she had a to-do list that would drive most people her age to retire to their recliners.

There were friends to visit, nourishing food to be cooked and delivered, gossip to be exchanged, advice to be offered, knitting to be needled, planning to be done. For Mrs. Stedman busy was good, busy made time fly, busy kept her up to snuff.

It had been a long, cold, winter. She was stomping through the snow on her way home. Stomping kept her warm and she liked the nice scrunchy sound her boots made on the snow. Most of

3

all it gave her a satisfying sense of defiance in the face of the endless, dreary weather.

She was carrying a bag of carefully selected items purchased at her favorite local Deli: chocolate bits and dates, (Mr. Herman had hinted at a longing for her cookies), a small chicken and a few veggies (soup of course) and a packet of a new tea called Spice Heaven ("A lemon and raspberry blend for a Restful lift" It advertised), and the latest Psychology Today, (Mrs. Stedman liked to keep up, she prided herself for the quality of the advice she dispensed.)

With a few last off-with-the-snow stomps she marched through the lobby of her apartment building picking up her mail as she headed up to her apartment.

With automatic efficiency she took off her cloth coat and red knitted hat, carefully hanging them up. Then tugging off her boots, she slipped on her well-worn, cozy slippers. She dropped the mail by her chair, then brewed herself a cup of Spice Heaven tea and eased her small roundish body into her big comfortable chair with a happy sigh to enjoy a few sips of her new tea. (not bad she thought, Mr. Herman might like a few bags to go with his cookies.) As she skipped through her mail she was surprised to find a letter from her daughter Anna.

Anna had recently made arrangements for her mother to fly to California for a visit. She was moving into a new condo. She wanted her mother to see it and, while there, enjoy some time in San Francisco. Mrs. Stedman wondered what Anna was writing about now. Maybe she wanted her to bring a few of her favorite New York delicacies, or maybe suggesting the clothes she should bring. She carefully opened the envelope, smoothed out the page, and started to read.

Dear Mom,

I'm really looking forward to your visit, I'm dying to show you my new condo. Unfortunately, I had some disappointing news this afternoon. The symphony office is sending me to Denver for three days, there just isn't a realistic way to get out of it. I'm really sorry about those first few days, but we'll have plenty of time when I get back.

I hope you don't mind mom, I've booked you into a beautiful beach resort. Actually, after such a bad winter back there, a little restful beachcombing and bird watching might be a happy way to spend those few days that I'm away.

Can't wait to see you, Love, Anna

Mrs. Stedman put the letter its envelope and rested her head on the chair pillow. Why not, she thought, there won't be much to keep me busy, but Anna will be back soon. Visions of restful days and cozy nights, accompanied by a roaring surf, filled her mind as she dozed off.

As Mrs. Stedman stepped off the shuttle bus her senses seemed to compete for her attention. Everything around her seemed to sparkle in the clear, warm, sunlight. The sea smell, the roar of the surf beyond the dunes, the stunning white egrets, tensely motionless as they stared purposefully at the marsh water just across the road. Anna was right, she thought, this is a beautiful spot!

Slowly she turned and went inside to register. Waiting in line at the reception desk Mrs. Stedman had an opportunity to check out her fellow guests. Most of them appeared to be men in their thirties she thought. Many of them apparently knew each other. She decided there must be some sort of meeting going on. Then her thoughts moved on. I wonder where the nearest market might be? Her condo was to have its own kitchen. With all the time she'd have, she planned to try a few new recipes - maybe even freeze some things to take up to Anna.

"Mrs. Stedman" she announced as she stepped up to the counter.

"Welcome Mrs. Stedman," said the friendly young receptionist. you are in Shorebirds 192. Here's your packet and key, the Welcome Meeting is scheduled for three o'clock at the Lagoon House. "Grand" said Mrs.

Stedman. "It's always such a friendly touch to have a welcome get-together. I'll be there."

Once in her condo she started to look around. Of particular interest was the small kitchen. "Well equipped" she murmured as she touched the handsome blue electric mixer on the counter and the new coffee maker. The cupboard was full of pots and pans.

The kitchen opened into a cozy living room with a fireplace and comfortable seating. There was a big, framed, bird chart over the book case, and nearby she found a stereo. She turned it to a classical music station, then headed to the window to open the blinds. Sun, and the intense blue of the sea and sky, poured in as the blinds went up. Right in front of her hypnotic waves rolled slowly, thoughtfully, into dramatic peaks, then crashed into swirling pools of bubbles. Busy children played with buckets in the sand while moms chatted and dads threw frisbies. She stood there gazing out, unable to tear herself away.

Then, to her surprise, she found that there was yet another door off the living room. It was another bedroom with its own private bathroom and the same fabulous ocean view.

"Why in the world would Anna have rented a two bedroom?" she wondered. "Way too extravagant," she quietly scolded. "I'll have to speak to her about it." For now though she shrugged, moved to the front bedroom and started to unpack. She started by taking out a treasured picture of Anna playing a flute solo with the San Francisco Symphony. She polished it lovingly and placed it next to her bed.

Waking up early as usual, Steven stretched, hit the radio's snooze alarm, and settled back into the pillows. The positive energy of a Vivaldi violin concerto intertwined with the sun streaming into the window. It's a day for the coast route south he thought as he stretched his long limbs and rolled out of bed. If I have to go to this company seminar, I might as well at least enjoy the trip down there.

Steven dressed and packed carefully for the meeting, designer-label casual. He looked at ease in his teal Gap sport shirt and Polo khaki pants. His normally unruly brown hair was carefully styled, Cole Haan loafers appropriately old and perfectly polished, completed the desired look. He ate his cereal standing in the sun at the window, then watered a couple of appreciative plants, grabbed his bags and headed out. He threw the duffel bag in the trunk of the Saab, then carefully settled his violin case to the side.

"What a joke" he mused as he backed out of the driveway, "I've worked so hard to perfect the role of Promising-Mr.-Management, yet the closer I get the less comfortable it feels. None of it is really me."

It was a five-star day as he headed south. Steven banished all further thoughts of business. He just wanted to enjoy the day's drive. It was a feast of clear, bright colors: fields covered with yellow mustard, intense orange poppies, and sweeping green hills dotted with reddish-brown cows silhouetted against the startling blue sky. Red-tail hawks shopped for lunch from lofty lookouts. The ocean was an ever-changing drama of calm and excitement.

As Steven neared Santa Cruz his thoughts returned to the seminar. With a sinking sense of depression. "God", he thought, "I've been to so many of these damn meetings. They are always the same. Everyone trying to out shine the others. Schmoozing up to management, posturing for each other, eating and drinking too much. It's like summer camp without the fun, a bunch of anxious kids showing off.

It was but a short jump from those thoughts to musing about his life in general. Things had been going pretty well really. After five years with the company he'd relaxed into the job. The work was still boring but at least it wasn't so stressful now, kind of comfortable really. Best of all he finally had some free time. He'd gone on some good camping trips, really enjoyed some cooking classes, and was looking forward to an up-coming river-rafting trip. The best thing though was that he had found time for his real love, music. His violin had always been a special inspiration and comfort to him. Now, finally, he was practicing again and loving it.

His mind drifted on, then bumped to a halt. "Yeah," he admitted to himself, "there's still something missing." It had been a long time since he'd had an on-going relationship. He wondered why. Too busy he thought. "No that's not it. I just haven't met anyone even tempting." There'd been a couple of times when he'd met a woman who seemed worth a try, but in the end, it had always seemed like more work than the project merited.

"Well" he thought as he drove through the gates of The Dunes, "At least this beautiful place is always a treat. Maybe this time there will be a cool woman at the conference to beach walk with."

"Shorebirds 192" the desk clerk said handing him his key'

"Will I be sharing my condo with anyone this year" he asked?

Looking at her clipboard, she announced that there was a woman assigned to the other room.

Stevens head shot up. "Really!" Things were looking up already.

"Has she checked in yet?" he asked.

"She checked in about an hour ago."

It was tempting to blurt out "What did she look like" but he let that one pass. He headed for the door. I'll find out for myself.

Steven decided to knock before using his key. After all, the space had been hers for the last hour or so. It would be a better start moving in after introductions.

A knock, a short wait, and the door opened. A comfortable looking older woman with decidedly grey hair opened the door. She was wearing blue polyester pants and a matching tunic with flamboyant metallic swirls. They stood there staring at each other.

Finally, with a warm smile, she asked if he was looking for someone.

Steven looked from his key, to the door, to the woman in front of him.

"I think there's been a mistake." he said. As each of them explained their presence at room 192 the situation became clear, somehow Mrs. Stedman had been shuffled on to the seminar roster.

Cordially she invited Steven into "her" condo, assuring him that she'd have it all straightened out shortly.

Picking up the phone, she called the front desk. In her usual, crisp friendly manner she explained their dilemma. Half an hour later the two of them sat in the living room dicussing their options. There were, she'd been told, absolutely no other rooms. The office was terribly sorry, they would be happy to refund her money but, other than that there was nothing they could do. Mrs. Stedman and Steven eyed each other with a new kind of appraisal.

"Why not," thought Mrs. Stedman, it would actually be kind of nice to have someone around. Three days could be a long time all by myself. We each have our own bedroom and bath, he looks like a nice young man.

Oh heck, Steven thought. At least I won't be living with a bunch of juvenile, drunken, jerks. Why not, he thought, she seems pleasant enough.

OK they agreed, let's give it a try.

Mrs. Stedman decided to pass up the Welcome Party. Clearly it wasn't the sort of get-acquainted evening she'd anticipated. Instead she took the shuttle bus to a local grocery to stock the condos cute little kitchen. Out of the blue she'd been handed the gift of someone to worry about. That evening when Anna called to make sure her mother had settled in comfortably, Mrs. Stedman happily replied that she was having considerably more fun than she'd expected. When Steven got back that evening he found milk and cookies by his bed. The issue never came up again.

The next morning, Steven got up at 8:00 for the 8:30 meeting. He ran over to the meeting room, choked down questionable coffee and a sickeningly sweet donut as he ran through the lobby to the meeting.

The next morning he gratefully accepted breakfast on the balcony with Mrs. Stedman. Perfect sweet Italian coffee, eggs, bacon, homemade biscuits with marmalade. They chatted about their lives — actually Steven did most of the talking while Mrs. Stedman smilingly murmured encouraging comments, poured more coffee, offered more biscuits, and asked the occasional, interested, question. Steven didn't get to the meeting until nearly ten but somehow it just didn't seem to matter. That evening he asked if she'd like to try a local fish restaurant with him. "Yes indeed, she'd love to."

During dinner. she shared that she'd called home earlier in the day to check on her friend Mr. Herman. He'd mentioned an old friend, a retired violinist in San Francisco, who teaches master classes. He's always looking for new talent Mrs. Stedman mentioned thoughtfully. Steven gratefully accepted the name and address offered.

The next evening as Steven sat through a mandatory after dinner meeting, he realized how much he was looking forward to getting back to Shorebirds 192. Somehow his visits with Mrs. Stedman felt more real to him than the endless marketing and sales meetings. "Who really cares" he thought to himself as the latest innovations were heralded in multimedia at the podium.

Later, as he let himself into the condo, he found Mrs. Stedman relaxing in a big chair, looking out at the moon on the water.

"Ah" she greeted him, "I was hoping you might be back in time to serenade me this evening. Did you bring your violin with you by any chance?"

I always take it with me when I can," he admitted. It was carefully stowed in his room. He started with a few familiar warm-up pieces. Then, moved by the comfort of the moment and the beautiful evening, he played on and on, lost in the music. Mrs. Stedman was genuinely moved, gently clapping for encores, commenting on the different pieces, encouraging him to continue.

As he started to play the beautiful melody from Beethoven's Second Romance, his glance fell on a framed picture on the coffee table. a young woman playing a flute. There was something about the picture that held his attention, the woman seemed to fill the picture with the joy of what she was doing, dreamy, yet alert, concentrating yet beyond the details. The beauty of the moment captured was startling. As he continued to play he began to feel like he was playing to, almost with, the woman looking out at him.

When he finished the piece, he continued to gaze at the face in the frame. Mrs. Stedman said nothing. Finally, he asked if the picture was hers or if it had been in the condo all along. Mrs. Stedman casually said that it was her daughter Anna.

"Would you play the Beethoven again, Please?"

As Steven went to bed that night his mind was full of the face in the picture. He tried to remember what Mrs. Stedman had told him about Anna's life but he realized that he'd actually done most of the talking. Who was she? Where was her daughter, what did Anna do? His dreams that night were of himself chasing an elusive woman, the woman in the picture, playing his violin magnificently as he ran after her.

At breakfast the next morning Mrs. Stedman mentioned that she'd be leaving the next day. She was taking the shuttle back to the airport, then she and Anna would take a taxi on to San Francisco. She chatted enthusiastically about Anna's new apartment and visiting The City.

Steven knew that the conference was over as far as he was concerned.

"How about a trip to Monterey today," he asked as if it was a casual thought. He needed time with Mrs. Stedman. He felt possessed by the need to know more about Anna. As the day progressed however, they enjoyed sightseeing, and spent time at the aquarium. They had lunch on Cannery Row. Mrs. Stedman said little about Anna, yet everything she did say seemed to whet his appetite for more.

That night Mrs. Stedman called Anna to say that a young man she'd met had offered to drive her to the airport and then would drive the two of them on up to San Francisco.

They were driving back up the coast. "Let's roll the windows down," Mrs. Stedman suggested, "I'd like to experience this scenery completely." She was taking it all in, cheerfully commenting about everything she saw.

Steven answered absently, lost in another reverie about his life. As the wind tousled his hair and warmed his face he reflected on how different . . . how carefree actually . . .he was feeling. He had a totally different sense of himself than he'd had on the trip south just three days ago. Without much thought, and with no regret, his demanding Mr. Management role had been left somewhere at the dunes. He was leaving the seminar two days early and it was of no concern to him what-so-ever. His career seemed to have faded into a distant fog.

Full of light and clarity, he looked forward to meeting Mr. Herman's friend. "The time is right," he said to himself. "I'm going to move seriously toward my dream as a professional musician."

At the airport Steven suggested that Mrs. Stedman stay with the car so that they wouldn't have to park. He'd run in to meet Anna.

"How will you know her?" Mrs. Stedman asked.

"I'd know her anywhere" was thrown over his shoulder as he took off. Mrs. Stedman sat in the car smiling comfortably.

Finally, she saw Anna, long legs striding gracefully, long auburn hair floating around a wide grin. Steven was behind her with her garment bag.

As Anna saw her mother she winked, then hugged her as she whispered, "You've been busy haven't you Mom." Mrs. Stedman smiled and shrugged.

The car turned out of the airport and started north. Mrs. Stedman sat in the back, "so she could rest." In the front seats Steven and Anna were lost in an animated get-acquainted conversation.

"A wonderful vacation, thought Mrs. Stedman. Providence had given her something special to do and, actually it had been so easy. It might well turn out to have been some of her best work yet. She smiled as she dozed off "Busy is good" she murmured to herself.

Living Our Lives

Pillow - Best . . . $2.50

I t was 1930 - Ginnie and Ev had known each other all their lives. As kids they'd gleefully fought over endless childish disputes, Slowly the battles turned into heart to heart confidences. Finally, on graduation night, they'd become lovers in the back of Uncle John's borrowed roadster. There was no question that they would marry, but they decided to wait until they had saved up a nest egg. Ginnie didn't mind waiting. She enjoyed working at Mr. Hodges Insurance office and she waitressed four nights a week at the Downtown Diner. The other three nights belonged to Ev. Ev worked at the farm supply store and helped his dad on the farm. His real love was music. Whenever he had the time he taught music lessons.

One hot summer day after work Ev and Ginnie biked out to the river with a group of friends. They spent the afternoon sliding down the huge, wet, boulders to swim in the cold pools below. The afternoon always ended with a wild water fight. Cool and happy they would lie around chatting and , enjoying their cold beer and watermelon.

Slowly the others began to drift off to other evening plans. Ev and Ginnie stayed by the river. Spreading out an old blanket, Ginnie had stretched out, and was gazing up at the old cottonwood trees dancing in the breeze. Ev got out his fiddle and began to play.

"What's that you're playing Ev?" Ginnie asked.

"It's a Scottish song," he answered, "The braw lads o' Galla Water." He looked down at her and smiled. She looked so beautiful lying there on the green blanket, her red hair spread out around her face. He started to play another Robert Burns song.

'O, my love is like a red, red rose,

that's newly sprung in June.

O, my love is like a melody

that sweetly plays in tune.

Ev stopped playing and looked at Ginnie for a long time. Finally, he put his fiddle down beside him. "Ginnie," he began slowly, "My mom and dad told me this morning that they've decided to move up to Oregon. Dad has been offered a job there." Again, there was a long pause. "They said we could have the farm Ginnie." Ev was picking up speed and confidence. "It's not much but it could be a start, at least until I can teach full time." he paused, "Maybe you could go on working for a little while?" I can paint the house, they are leaving most of the furniture."

Ev looked straight into Ginnie's green eyes. "Marry me Ginnie. Mary me now. I want us to be together."

"Of course I'll marry you Ev." Ginnie was laughing. Yes! Yes! Yes! Together they rolled on the blanket in a joyful mutual YES!

There was no reason to wait any longer. Two weeks later they were married on the lawn of what would soon be their new home. As the evening of dancing and singing, eating and toasting, wound down Ev and Ginnie left for a weekend away on their own. Uncle John had lent them his roadster once again. They returned on Sunday to the empty house they found a note anchored by a tall jar of roses.

"May you be as happy here as we have been. We love you, Mom and Dad."

Ginnie had visited Ev's home many times. It had always felt warm and welcoming though on the low side of modest. It had been a happy home full of music and busy activities and laughter. Now it seemed rather empty and sad. Ginnie walked thoughtfully through the tiny house. Her favorite feature was the covered front porch. She settled herself on the porch swing with her list of ideas and plans. She wanted to make the house their own. The next day she brought home a Sears Roebuck catalogue. She and Ev spent the evening poring over the catalogue's offerings. Slowly "nice ideas" were dropped and a much shorter list of "needs" developed. One thing Ginnie insisted on was new bedding. Carefully they decided on a serviceable wool blanket, a set of cotton sheets that she planned to embroider when she had time, and a cornflower blue chenille bed spread.

Finally, they turned to the pillows. They were marked "good," "better," "best." Without discussion Ginnie wrote "Best, top quality, with blue and white ticking," on the order form. "I've saved enough to cover all this," Ginnie announced. "A good night's sleep is important. I don't want to scrimp on pillows. They will need to last for a long time." She put the order and a check in an envelope to mail the next day.

A friend and I were suddenly grabbed from a Sears Roebuck shelf. We were stuffed into a card board box. The box was sealed, and a label was slapped on. We were off to a new life in Northern California.

After a long stuffy trip, we were finally delivered to a small but cheerful house. An excited young woman met us at the front door, almost hugging the mailman as she thanked him. She closed the door and turned to rush up the stairs, pulling at the mailing tape as she went. She went into the small bedroom and dropped the package on the bed. Eagerly she took my box-mate out first. She gave it a good hug and squeeze, then placed it on the bed. Next, she pulled me out, patting and fluffing me before placing me next to my friend. Then she laid me down and wiggled a bit to get it just right. "You're mine," she said, "you're perfect." Turning to the window she called out with a laugh, "Ev, our new pillows have come!"

I lived with Ginnie and Ev for about 20 years. They were good times. There was always music in the house and Ginnie took good care of us. Always clean linens, and always a happy sigh when her head settled on me at night. Ev would pull his pillow over next to me. They'd lie there, talking and kissing,

I loved the slow excitement as they made love.

I remember hard times too, like when she Ginnie lost their first expected baby. Ginnie almost drowned me with her tears. Sometime after that she had an almost fatal case of the flu. My most exciting moment, was when she delivered the most wonderful little girl. The midwife swaddled the small body and handed it back to Ginnie, laying the little head snuggled into Ginnie's arm. "Come say hello to Annie," Ginnie called to Ev. The three of them lay there in a glow of happiness.

Eighteen years later the family was preparing to drive Annie down to U.C. Berkeley where she'd received a music scholarship. Annie packed her carefully chosen wardrobe, along with special books and precious pictures into the car. Just before leaving, Ginnie ran back into the house and returned with me under her arm.

"I want you to have this pillow," she told Annie, "It saw you born, it should be with you now that you will be on your own."

Annie laughed, "You're so silly Mom." But she was hugging me as we drove away.

In 1955 Annie met Tom, a tall handsome man with dark curly hair, warm brown eyes, and a remarkable smile. They studied together and dated for quite a while before Tom was suddenly drafted for the Korean war. They decided to marry before he left. I, of course, was with them on their last night. It was a night to remember. All night long they talked, and laughed and cried, and mostly made love over and over again. I was on the floor, I was on one end of the bed, then the other, and then under Annie. I was dizzy by the time they finally slept for the hour or two before Tom had to leave. It was lucky I was with Annie. She talked to me at night, and read me Tom's letters. I held and comforted her when the letters didn't come. Sometimes she would toss and turn all night, shoving me every which way trying to find comfort and rest.

When Tom returned we moved to a little tract home south of San Francisco. Annie and Tom fixed it up slowly. Piece by piece they chose their new Danish Modern furniture. Annie decided it was time for new bedding. I was naturally concerned, but I understood. In a soft white pillow case I was moved to the guest room. I was comfortable, but it wasn't very exciting.

One day, quite suddenly, Tom rushed in and grabbed me. He ran out to the car and shoved me through the window onto Annie's lap. Annie was very pregnant, we were racing to the hospital. "I wouldn't go without you" she told me. "You were there when I arrived, I want you to be one of the first to see *my* baby." And sure enough, when the nurses and doctors finally left, Tom, Annie, and I sat on the bed holding Julie. What a special moment it was. I had a grand surprise when Ev and Ginnie came down to meet Julie. When Ginnie climbed into bed the first night she lay back with a happy sigh. After a minute or so she sat up again.

"Ev," she exclaimed. "This is my wonderful pillow." How grand it was that she remembered me.

It was 1975 Tom had signed up as a volunteer to help restore an old Liberty ship in San Francisco, Usually he would go up every week to work on the old treasured steam engine. He enjoyed talking to the visitors that came aboard; old seamen, young people interested in the ship's history, wide eyed little kids. Occasionally he would spend the night on the ship if he was in the middle of a project. He'd always take his own pillow to ensure a good night's sleep.

Now he was at home resting on the couch. All of a sudden there was a yelp from the laundry room. "Tom, you left my special pillow on the ship, you brought back the wrong one!" Tom shrugged, "Sorry Annie, I'll get it next week." Actually, it was like a little vacation and an interesting adventure for me.

When Tom brought me home Annie and Julie met me at the front door. Julie, with great excitement, announced that she too accepted by U.C. Berkeley. With the car full of her "necessities", Annie and Tom drove Julie up to help her get comfortable and organized in her dormitory. Finally, when it was time to leave, Annie took me out of a shopping bag and settled it on her bed with a little note. "My pillow is yours now Julie. Treat it well, it's been a good friend of mine." Don't worry Mom, Julie said, "we'll be just fine."

It was 1981. After graduation Julie had gone to work at a rising Silicon Valley company. She met Mike while working together on numerous projects. As time went by they found they enjoyed similar interests and enjoyed being together. Mike was an easy-going man, open and interested in seemingly everything. He was comfortable with himself, making it easy to feel that you'd always known him.

One beautiful day they decided to take a day off. Santa Cruz was their choice of destinations. They knew it wouldn't be swarming with day to trippers the way it usually is on weekends. The perfect get-away day. They spent time on the Mall window shopping, then took a break to enjoy coffee, and special pastries at an outside table... the perfect place for people-watching. From there they took off for a long walk along West Cliff Drive. They stopped to watch the surfers, chatted with locals, and petted good looking dogs. Mike suggested they stay late enough to watch the sun go down and then have dinner on the pier.

It had been clear for some time that they planned to marry, it just always felt like they were too busy, or for some reason the timing was wrong. Now, as they had recently been offered jobs in Seattle, it felt like it was the perfect time to make it happen. They wanted to marry before they left so their friends and family could be with them. At dinner they sat under a bright starry sky. Ideas and plans flowed easily with help from a considerable amount of champagne. They drove home with their simple wedding plans decided.

The next day Julie spent the day packing and piling the boxes in the corner. It was a hot, sticky afternoon. Damp and tired she grabbed a coke from the fridge and wandered out onto her balcony. She ruffled her short, dark, damp, hair in the breeze, then stretched out on the chaise. I was there because Julie used to read out there. She'd tuck me under her neck.

When Mike arrived with a bottle of wine and sandwiches he came out on balcony and settled himself on the chaise, Julie sat in on an old wicker chair beside him with her feet up on the chaise. They sat there chatting, slowly enjoying the wine and sandwiches. After a while Julie grinned at Mike, "You're looking way too yummy lying there." She stood up, swung her leg over the chaise and sat on Mike's lap. In the cool evening breeze, they kissed and spoke softly to each other. Languorously they made love under the stars, then slept there all tangled up together with their heads on me.

I was an old pillow then. I wore a colorful pillow case, but my blue and white ticking was faded and stained. Some of my feathers were still in good shape, but most had congealed into lumpy little knots. The next morning, I wondered what Julie was thinking as she gazed at me. "You've been around as long as I can remember." She picked me up and we danced around the balcony for a bit. She seemed to be feeling me carefully, thoughtfully. Finally, she went into the kitchen and came back with a pair of scissors and a big plastic bag. She carefully undid one of my seams, then reached in took all of my good, fluffy, feathers and put them in the black bag so that none of them would be lost. Then she took the blue and white ticking and turned it upside down over the balcony. Those feathers flew out, whirling and gliding they fell to the ground. I couldn't help noticing that there were birds almost standing in line to collect the precious feathers for their nests.

Was I gone? No, not at all, my soul and history were in the black bag.

It was 1985. Ginnie and Annie had come up to Seattle to help Julie when the new baby was born. The doctor had told Julie it was a girl, and she was thrilled. "We're naming her Lisa", Julie told her mother and grandmother. Like Annie, Lisa was born at home and Mike helped with the birth. Lisa arrived quickly and cheerfully, it wasn't long before Mike rushed out to the lawn where Ginnie and Annie were waiting. With great excitement he announced that Julie wanted them to come in to meet Lisa.

Lisa's head lay on a small pillow in the crook of her mother's arm. As the "Oooh's" and "how sweets," and the hugs and tears of joy began to subside, Julie carefully pulled the little pillow from under Lisa's head. "I want you to see this" she said. It was me, the best of me, covered with an embroidery that Julie had finished just in time. On the front it said, "To Ginnie, Annie and Lisa, I have loved and cared for you all." Then Julie pointed out that there was room for more names as well.

I was in the middle of all the excitement. It felt fitting that I was there. After all I had seen, and been part of, their lives, for more than half a century. I felt privileged to have witnessed the intimate private moments of their lives. I had always helped as best I could. I'm smaller now and I spend most of my time on a rocker in Lisa's room. I rest and think about my memories. Lisa seems to understand that I am a member of the family. She treats me carefully. I expect to be around to welcome her grandchildren too.

Living Our Lives

In This Together

As Sarah hopped off the bus, just around the corner from Grove Lane, a wave of "almost home" enveloped her. The sturdy old maple trees were dispatching red and gold leaves of welcome that spun and floated down around her. Lost in the moment she spun and floated with them for a bit, then jumped into the neatly-piled leaves in front of her old home. She'd looked forward to this day. She always enjoyed visiting with her Mom and Grandmother. Nervously, excitedly, she'd decided this would be the perfect time to tell them her news.

Sarah and Andy had been living together for a couple of years. The company they'd worked for had moved out of town, they'd decided to go with it even though it would be hard, leaving their friends and families.

Sarah had made a point of staying in close touch with her Mom and Grandmother. There'd been lots of long phone calls, but it wasn't the same. Today was a special treat.

Turning into the driveway she tucked the bouquet of flaming chrysanthemums she'd brought for her mother under her arm. Then she quickly ran her fingers through her long blond hair and smoothed her patterned skirt and loose red sweater. With her warm open smile and graceful stride, she walked up the side of the house. She knew they'd be in the kitchen.

Her Mom, Joan, was at the door with a big hug. Across the room her grandmother, Emma, was setting the table. Smiling at Sarah she blew a kiss across the kitchen. Sarah elaborately caught it, then rushed to deliver it back to Emma with a hug.

At first the conversation rolled around the room with the this and that of catch-up news, but slowly there became a strange, disconcerting, silence that settled over the three of them. Sarah was arranging her flowers, Joan, busied herself with lunch preparations, and Emma was fussing with the table. Instinctively Sarah knew that they too had something they wanted to discuss. She placed the flowers on the table, then moved around the room touching familiar objects: a lovely old copper teapot, pictures of graduations, several of her mother's glass animals.

Emma helpfully broke the silence;

"What are you and Andy planning to do to your new house?"

With a sense of a reprieve Sarah launched into the subject; discussing remodeling plans, colors, important details filled the empty places in the conversation.

Suddenly, as if she had planned this very moment for days, Joan leapt in with the question Sarah had hoped to avoid.

"But Sarah," she said, "Just what kind of a commitment is buying a house together?"

Joan brushed back her hair and looked straight at Sarah. Emma was looking at her too. Joan went on with obvious expectation in her voice, "Are you talking about marriage."

Sarah and Andy had been together for three years. Joan couldn't understand why they weren't taking the next step.

Sarah was looking down, fiddling with her napkin. Finally, she murmured,

"No, we're not talking about marriage, but I'm pregnant."

Holding her breath Sarah caught the startled glance between Joan and Emma. The next moment the three of them rushed to each other as if pulled by a common thread. Hugging and laughing at the unexpected turn of events. With new excitement the three of them talked over lunch: When? How was Sarah feeling, what arrangements had they made? But once the again, the real question came up.

"Doesn't this mean you'll be getting married" Joan asked again.

Sarah looked at her plate, unhappily on the spot. Emma thoughtfully stepped in again. "What is it about marriage that seems to worry you both so much?" Sarah gazed at the two wonderful, important women in her life, then side-stepped the issue.

"Was it really all that simple for the two of you?"

Emma spoke first, "It was so different back then. In the framework of my up-bringing, marriage was the definition of happiness. I'd known your grandfather all my life. We enjoyed each other, he had a good job in his father's business, and he treated me like a princess.

34

I couldn't imagine it being any better. It was a good marriage"

She ended with a remembering kind of smile.

Joan sat back in her chair wrestling with her own decision to marry. She and her high school sweetheart had spent hot, steamy nights at the Redwood Drive-in doing everything possible except "it." She'd not planned to marry right away, she'd wanted to travel, maybe work for a while first. But Sex = love = marriage back then. "I knew I sure wanted George physically, so I figured it meant I was in love with him. There were ups and downs, but all in all it was a good, comfortable, marriage."

Emma and Joan turned to Sarah, and now it's your turn. As Sarah tried to arrange her thoughts the doorbell rang. Gratefully she jumped up and hurried off to open the door.

"Andy said he'd come by to pick me up after lunch."

As they came back into the kitchen Emma and Joan regarded Andy's easy smiling face, tousled brown hair and green eyes with obviously enhanced interest.

"It's Andy's turn", Sarah thought to herself, *"maybe he can make sense of our fears and uncertainties better than I can."* Without ceremony she threw the question to him, "They want to know why we're not talking about getting married."

Suddenly on the spot, Andy settled on a straight-forward approach. "I love Sarah too much to have our relationship messed up with the have-to's and ought-to's of marriage, the last thing we want is to spoil the wonderful relationship we share now."

Andy continued, speaking of their many friends who had broken up after having deciding to marry. Suddenly Andy realized that the perfect answer was sitting in his car.

"Hey Sarah," he grinned, "I've got something for you. It was for later actually, but I think I'll just get it now."

Joan and Emma smiled at Sarah as he went outside. "He's such a nice young man Sarah, he obviously cares a lot for you."

Andy returned with an expression that was half-pleased-with- himself, half embarrassed uncertainty. He deposited a huge, beautifully wrapped box on Sarah's lap. Carefully she opened the package and lifted out a large stuffed bear with a blue ribbon around its neck. Hanging on the ribbon was an enormous fake diamond ring. The whole room seemed to stop breathing as Sarah opened the bear's card. Slowly, quietly, she read the card aloud.

"Andy and baby and I know we want you in our lives forever. Marry us Sarah, We love you. Andy"

All eyes were on Sarah hugging the soft snugly bear. "I don't know she whispered, it's still scary. On the other hand," she looked at Andy as she moved her hand to her tummy, "I can feel a baby that has made an enormous commitment to the two of us. I know, you Andy, I love and trust you more than anything." Laughing she turned to Joan and Emma, "And you know I feel your love and support all through me - always."

She paused, then taking the blue ribbon and ring from the bear's neck and put it around her own, "If this obviously wisest of bears can say 'forever' then so can I." She turned happily to Andy, 'Yes" she said, "It's time. Let's do it. There are too many of us in this together to turn back now."

"A wedding!" Emma and Joan were beside themselves, "And a baby too! What can we do to help?" Andy, Sarah and the bear were hugging. "Don't worry," Sarah smiled at them over Andy's shoulder "We'll call you tomorrow."

Living Our Lives

Flight From Perfect to Happy

I know that planning a perfect wedding is just a matter of efficient planning and organization.

It's Thursday today, Mike and I will be married on Sunday. I came in to work early so I could go over everything one more time. It looks like I have covered almost everything.

My name is Lyn. I'm 28, I work at a large Silicon Valley company. Our perfect wedding is going to be on Sunday. I'm almost done with the details. I sit back and think about it all. I get all emotional just thinking about it.

I smooth out my well-tailored blue pantsuit, stretch, then pull my auburn hair into a comfortable ponytail. I close my eyes and dreamily picture the wedding.

Just as I start straightening my desk my cool boss, Jim, walks in. He and I have worked together for ever. It's an easygoing relationship, lots of teasing and fun along with the work.

"'Do I get to walk you down the aisle?" he asks.

"In your dreams" I answer with a grin. "Anything else you'd like?"

"Well yes," there was a pause, "Actually, I just had a call from Vancouver. They've settled on a date for your presentation. I know this isn't great timing Lyn, but we need this sale. They want us, actually you, to be there at 9 o'clock Friday morning."

My head was reeling, "Vancouver . . . this Friday? . . . You're kidding! . . . aren't you?" There was a short silence I realize he's serious.

"My God Jim, we're getting married on Sunday. I have heaps to do before then. On the other hand, this project is mine, my research, my baby, my presentation. I can't just hand it over to someone else."

Jim looked miserable. "I'm sorry Lyn, I tried my best to negotiate another time but this was our time slot. they're interviewing several companies. We have two options, I could go for you, but I know you are far more familiar with the material, or you go and trust that the wedding will be perfect whether you're agonizing about it or not"

I was pouting, verging on tears actually, I was rummaging around in my desk drawer for a Kleenex.

"OK, I'll go, but I'd better be home on Friday night, *no matter what!*"

"I'm sure you can do it," Jim nodded, I know you'll be home in time, I promise."

Jim left. I stared at myself in the little wall mirror near my desk. My long, simple, satin wedding gown floated into the image. It's perfect I thought again. I love the way that it exaggerates my height. I'm almost as tall as my handsome groom Mike. My mother calls it statuesque, Mike calls it sexy. I draw my hair back and up as it will be for the wedding.

"Okay, quit stalling," I say to myself. I pull myself back, "I need to call Mike." I can picture him answering the phone at his huge old desk. He'll be looking out the window as he leans back and rumples his thick dark hair. He's an outdoors kind of guy, tall and muscular. He never really seems comfortable in his office chair. I think he'll be furious that Jim even asked me to go.

I think to myself, *"Okay Lyn, get yourself together."* It's important that I sound excited, I sure don't want to cry!

Finally, I dialed Mike and welcomed his warm "hello." I decide to launch right in. "Jim just came in with upsetting news Mike. He's asked me to go to Seattle on Friday. I know it's disappointing Mike but I feel I have to go. I've managed this project all along, and I'd really like to see it through. Jim promised I'd be back in time for the rehearsal on Friday."

There was a long silence, then

"Lousy timing that's for sure . . . but I do understand Lyn." Mike sounded uncertain, "We'd wanted to have time to enjoy the pre-wedding fun and relax and enjoy the festive build-up to the wedding. We wanted to have nothing unexpected or stressful to worry about." There was another long pause. Then, in a lighter tone, he went on, "Just take care of yourself Sweetheart. We'll deal with things here. Let me know when you will be getting in and I'll be at the airport."

I relaxed my grip on the receiver,

"Thanks Mike for understanding."

I hung up and took a deep breath. "Mike is so special," I thought again as I hung up.

The Seattle presentation was my best ever. They bought our product. I was so excited! At the same time, I was anxious to head home. As I was repacking my materials and thanking them for the contract. the whole group raised their water classes in a toast.

"Happy Wedding Lyn, Best of Luck!"

Then a secretary handed me the telephone. It's the airport she said as she handed me the phone.

A man's voice spoke. "Hello Lyn, my name is Tom Mathews. The airline pilots have voted to strike this morning. (Oh God, I just knew something like this would happen.") I didn't know what to say.

The man's warm, confident voice went on, "Jim called me this morning to ask if I would fly you down to Monterey. I'm at the airport's private plane area. Look for a blue and white Cessna 210. We're ready to take off as soon as you get here."

My heart sunk, a single engine plane? Luckily there wasn't time to dwell on it, I was out of the building and running for a taxi.

We pulled up to the gate. I leapt out looking for a blue and white plane. There was only one in sight. It looked like a tiny, shiny, insect. I was standing there looking at it when a fifty-something-ish, friendly guy walked up to me.

"I'm Tom, your pilot." Have you ever flown in a small plane before? You're going to love it." He had a great smile. "It's a beautiful day" he continued, "It will be easy going. We'll have you in Monterey in plenty of time for your wedding rehearsal."

His enthusiasm was catching. I pulled myself together and followed him over to the little plane. He helped me in, secured the door, then strode around to the other side and climbed in.

"Okay, all set for take-off. Tom helped me buckle myself in and handed me a set of earphones. He explained how they worked if I wanted to use the mic to talk to him. Finally, he pointed to a basket in the back.

"I've brought sandwiches, fruit, and some sodas in case we get hungry. Help yourself."

I found myself relaxing into Tom's confidence and obvious experience.

This just might be a fun adventure, I thought. I might as well enjoy it. Tom was going through a list of checks, and then we were speeding down the runway to suddenly lift off, climbing in a gentle arc.

Tom settled back, ran his fingers through his grey-streaked hair, and grinned. "We're on our way,"

As we flew Tom explained every maneuver and answered every question, he even predicted every bump. I relaxed into the beauty of the day and the scenery below. *I've flown a zillion times, yet it has never felt so free, so bird-like.* Having enjoyed a sandwich, I sat back and closed my eyes. My mind wandered, *I was Ingrid Bergman, I'm flying home from a dangerous mission. I'll be home soon to my dashing lover.*

When I woke we began to chat a bit. I asked Tom if he did much charter flying. He'd flown when he was in Vietnam and loved it. When he got home he bought the little Cessna plane. He enjoyed flying whenever he had the time. When Jim had called to see if he could fly Lyn to Monterey he was happy to help. . . and you too, he smiled at me.

"Jim lived in Monterey. He had two daughters around my age from a long-ago marriage."

"How about you?" he asked, "I understand there is a wedding Sunday."

I gushed about Joe. But then, most of all, I agonized about the wedding. "It can't possibly be perfect now" I wailed, "Lord, there so many things I still had scheduled to do."

"Who's walking you down the aisle?" Tom asked.

"My dad died when I was 15," I answered. "There really isn't anyone else I felt like asking. I'm a grown up, professional woman. I don't need anyone to give me away, I just decided to go it alone."

"You'll knock'em dead," he smiled.

Every so often Tom checked the instrument panel. As the engine hummed along he casually adjusted a knob here, flicked a switch there. Suddenly the engine gave a little hiccup. Tom's attention snapped back to the instrument panel. Carefully, intensely, he went over a drill of possibilities.

"Plenty of fuel," he muttered, "the fuel must be contaminated."

The engine stuttered a bit, then coughed. Then there was silence.

"We're going to have to land Lyn. Luckily, it's not too bad an area below. We'll find a reasonable place to land."

I can't believe it, this can't be happening! Jim promised me I'd be back . . . in one piece . . . in time for the wedding.

My heart was in my stomach. Staring out the window I could see that we were indeed going down, but at least we weren't dropping like a brick from the sky. We were gliding silently, circling in an easy spiral as Tom scanned for landing possibilities below. Finally, he pointed out a meadow just to the left. "That's it", he said, "I think that's the best we're going to find, and it's fairly flat and long enough."

Turning to me he added "Stay as calm as you can Lyn. Grab those jackets on the seat behind us. Just before we land I want you to put one over your face for protection, leave the other one next to my seat. All set?"

I nodded mutely, trying to remind myself to breath.

*'Please God, let me get home to Mike. Forget the perfect
wedding, just let me get home to Mike."*

We were almost down and on line to land. Up close the
meadow looked bumpy and dotted with bushes. Tom
appeared to be totally focused, and amazingly calm.
It could almost have been landing at the Monterey
airport.

"OK," Tom said, "Jacket up."

I could feel the wheels touch the ground. There was
a bounce, a lot of scratching noises, and a lurch to
the right. Then the little plane up-ended, nose to the
ground, and we stopped.

Tom looked over at me. I was struggling to straighten
up. I'd dropped the jacket and was hanging there,
looking down at a bush under the broken windshield.

"How are you doing Lyn?" Jim said.

"Fine thanks Tom, how about you?"

It sounded so casual, we both started to laugh.

Tears of laughter streamed down our faces as Tom tried
to help me with my seat belt. The belt suddenly let go
and I lurched forward, falling on a shard of window
glass. It sliced a gash right across my forehead. My
nervous laughter flipped. Hysterical tears of pain and
left-over fear took over. Tom helped me out of the

plane. He found a grassy spot so I could lie down and, rummaging around in his bag, found a clean tee shirt that he tied around my bloody forehead. Then he just held me until my sobs began to ebb. "It's OK Lyn, it's going to be OK."

Slowly we made our way across the meadow to a little country road that bordered the meadow. We sat there silently waiting.

Finally, an old Ford truck came down the road. Tom stood to wave it down, but it was stopping anyway.

"Hi there! Looks like you two are in some trouble,"

Turning down the loud music, a young teenager, dressed in jeans, a 4H shirt and an incongruous earring. He was grinning out the window at us.

"My name's Nate. Need some help?"

'That's our plane over there" Tom started. "We could really use a ride into town."

"Whoooeee!" exclaimed the young driver, "That must have been quite a ride! Come on, get in, I'll take you into Mount Shasta. There's a good clinic there."

Tom helped me into the truck, then climbed in next to me. While he and Nate chatted about the accident, I stewed about wedding plans that would have to be changed.

Nate dropped us off at the Clinic. As I was checking in Tom turned and gave me a big hug.

"Just let the doctor take care of that forehead now. I'll be back shortly."

Within half an hour Tom was back to pick me up. He'd rented a car, bought some sodas, and somehow found a blanket and pillow. Sporting 14 stitches and a large bandage around my head, I settled myself in the front seat. I smiled wanly at Tom. "You've been busy!"

Tom started the car and headed out to the highway.

"I have been busy" he told me. "I called Jim to tell him what happened and asked him to let Mike know. I thought you'd like to rest a little before talking to Mike yourself. We'll stop in Redding for a meal and you can call him from there. I also called the insurance company, they'll pick up the plane tomorrow. Sound OK?"

"OK with me, Tom, Thanks so much for all you've done."

I slept fitfully as we drove south. Dream bits swirling through my mind. The perfect wedding dress covered with blood, Bridesmaids looking all wrong because as I wasn't there to over-see it all, a frazzled bride watching the reception from a foggy distance. The jigsaw of my perfect wedding plans falling into disarray at my feet.

In Redding we stopped to eat and I called Mike. It felt so good to hear his voice, feeling his strength and love through the telephone.

I looked at Tom as we got back into the car.

"Gosh Tom, you must be absolutely exhausted. Can I drive for a while?"

From there on we took turns driving. When we were both awake we chatted about this and that, and what had happened, and of course I whined about the wedding again. Finally, Tom looked over at me and gave my hand a squeeze.

"Lyn, I really don't think you understand. Mike and your mother, and every one of your guests is going to be there because they love you. You could get married in a hay barn, in jeans, and they'd be happy. They'd love you just as much. Relax Lyn, it will all work out, in fact it's going to be wonderful. I know it!"

"Will you be there Tom? Will you please?"

Tears were welling up as a new thought formed in my mind.

"Will you walk me down the aisle?"

Tom laughed, hesitated, then got kind of misty himself.

Sure Lyn, I'll do it. I can't tell you how honored I am that you'd ask me."

then, with a grin, "will I be wearing my dirty tee shirt and jeans?"

We stopped in Sacramento so I could call Mike again. "Sweetheart, will you pick up another extra-large tux, and size 12 shoes. And please make sure there's a room for Tom."

We got to the resort where the wedding was to be late Saturday. Mike and Mom were waiting for us in the lobby. They were all over me as I got out of the car, asking questions, hugging, looking at my bandage. Finally, Mike turned to Tom

"Thanks Tom for all you've done, we all appreciate it so much! I've booked a room for you. I guess what you'd both like now is a bath and bed."

I got up late Sunday morning. Mom had arranged an afternoon of pampering and laughter with my bridesmaids at the day spa. When I was dressing for the wedding I realized that I wasn't the least bit interested in the details any more. I took Tom's word for it, it was all going to work out just right.

The guests were seated on the lawn, the bridesmaids walking slowly down the aisle. At the front Mike and the ushers were standing there smiling. As the string quartet started the first notes of "Here comes the bride". Mike suddenly raised his hand and the music stopped. Mike stepped forward.

"I'd like to tell you a story", he started. "My beautiful bride has just come through an incredible adventure. The private plane that was flying her back from an emergency trip to Seattle was forced to land in a field. Luckily the plane was piloted by an experienced and talented pilot, Tom Mathews. We are lucky to have them both with us today."

Mike stepped back and the music started again. Smiling at Tom I fluffed out my veil. It had cleverly been stitched to my bandage then circled with flowers. I took Tom's arm and we started down the aisle. On either side the standing guests reached out to us with their smiles and virtual hugs. Passing Jim, we winked at each other. I felt I was floating down the aisle on a great tide of love.

It was a perfect wedding. It was happiness, sharing, and celebrating our special moment with our families and friends. We ate, drank grateful toasts, and danced into the night. It couldn't have been more wonderful.

Finally, it was time for Mike and me to leave. As we went out the door we turned for a last look at the party. My eyes fell on a glowing twosome. It was my mom and Tom. "I think she was blushing," I said to Mike. Tom was standing next to her, his arm around her shoulder. With a great grin he gave us a happy thumbs up. Then they headed back to the dance floor.

Living Our Lives

Starting Over Again

Wearing her old, blue chenille bathrobe Joan sat slumped at the kitchen table. Face unwashed, hair uncombed, her face fallen with hopeless frustration. As she stared out the window doubts and dispair were beginning to take over again. She felt like everything she'd known had suddenly disappeared.

The final straw was her husband leaving recently for a younger woman at work.

Finally, with considerable effort, she straightened in her chair and pulled herself back to the present. She pulled back her auburn hair from her face and stretched. Shoving her coffee mug out of the way, she picked up the local newspaper and turned to the classified pages. Methodically her eyes moved up and down the columns. As always there wasn't a single listing that she qualified for, nor anything that sounded even slightly interesting, or payed more than minimum wage.

Joan had recently turned 40. Just a few years back, when her last child left for college, she'd decided to go back to the local University. With her family cheering her on, she'd proudly received her B.A.

Now as she folded the paper and tossed it into the recycle bin, she recalled that happy moment now with a bitter sense of irony. "A lot of good my degree's doing me now," she snarled. "Just what the heck do I do now?"

Old, annoying "all-you-have-to-do-is" ... advice danced a seductive reel in her head. "Be assertive!" "Sell yourself" "Do something you love and you'll prosper." It had been a month since her husband had left. She needed a job. Much more than that, she wanted a new life.

Finally, she got up and stretched. She added her mug to the dirty dishes in the sink and headed up the stairs. Passing her tiny study, she noticed a basket of old souvenirs and personal treasures she'd been sorting through. There, on the top of the pile, was a manila envelope with "JOAN" written on it in her grandmother's stylish handwriting. Inside there was a horoscope that Granny had had done the day Joan was born.

Joan sat down in her favorite rocker and picked up the horoscope. She hadn't looked at it in ages. "Maybe it will tell me what to do."

Scanning through the intricate star placement information and general characteristics, she finally found what she was looking for.

Joan should work in areas that use her strong intuition, it stated.

Suggested occupations:

Joan could be a fine surgeon. "Oh sure" she muttered.

Then, after several other unlikely suggestions, she saw, "Would be good at detective work."

Something clicked. She sat there for a moment picturing the idea. It was as if she'd just pushed a video tape into her head. A complete, detailed, fantasy unfolded. Travel, searching for interesting missing persons, helping people in distress, and yeah, why not, handsome, daring, fellow detectives. Joan put down the horoscope. Her eyes were shining as she searched for a local "Private Detective Agency" on her computer. She found there was one in town.

As Joan showered and dried her hair, the pros and cons chased each other around in her mind. "I wonder what's required beyond my "strong intuition. There must be training, I can handle that. What if I have to use a gun? I'm not really wild about seriously scary situations - let alone pain."

Putting all that aside, she pulled on her black slacks and a black turtleneck sweater. Giggling at the cat-burglar image in her full-length mirror. "Why not" she laughed," No harm in at least finding out about it."

She grabbed her purse and headed out the door with a feeling of lightness and excitement she hadn't felt in weeks.

Sandy Cross was a relatively small beach town. Not wanting to interrupt her momentum by bumping into anyone she knew. Joan discreetly parked down the street from the old office building on Front Street. Then she walked back and forth a bit to pluck up her nerve. Finally, with a deep breath, she went in. She studied the office directory, and found "Sure Help Detective Agency" on the third floor. A moment later she was knocking on the door. A low, bored, voice drawled, "Door's open."

The room was buried in books and papers. Dirty coffee mugs were used as paper weights. It was a dark room, yet what light there was seemed to glare directly on Joan. It took her a few seconds to focus on the man behind the desk. It was hard to tell how old he was, he looked disheveled and distracted, yet his clear, humorous eyes were disconcertingly studying Joan.

"My name is Joan Stevens," she started out. "I'd like to be a private detective. I've come to apply for a job." Darn she thought to herself, that was a really lame start!

"Why?" He tapped a pen on the desk as he answered. "I didn't advertise for anyone."

Joan considered how to answer why. "I know I'd be good at it," she said. Then, taking a deep breath, she squared her shoulders and looked him straight in the eyes. "I'm very intuitive, I'm good at reading people, and I'm... adventuresome." Then she sat back and studied her shoes as she waited him out. Some time passed before he leaned forward and looked at her with a little interest.

"Okay, good enough. His voice had a smoker's gravely quality.

After another long silence. "When can you start?"

"Well, I guess I... she stumbled in her confusion. I thought there would be a training period? Maybe testing? Some sort of license?"

He laughed at her as one might laugh at a three-year-old tripping over her own feet. Then, sitting up straight for the first time, he grabbed a card from a dirty bronze dish, and tossed it across the desk

Sure Help Private investigator.

"The best training is just doing it." he announced.

Then he slouched back in his chair again. Not much beyond that. Either you can do it or you can't. We'll see."

Joan stared at him.

"Like I said," Pete asked again. "When can you start?

I have something right now if you want it."

Well... Joan was stunned, yet at the same time excited and relieved. She stood up and beamed at Pete.

"I'm ready, she announced. What do I do? I'll start Monday, would that work out okay?"

"Fine." Pete pulled out a folder from his desk drawer, then wrote out a name and address. He described the case. It was a matter of Medicare fraud against a retirement home. Then he gave her the information she would need.

"Mrs. Shiffer is the sister of the retirement home owner. Think up a plausible reason for being there asking questions. Use an alias. Do your best to get whatever you can that might be useful and keep it light and friendly. Then, in a mocking tone as if he were addressing "Agent 007," he added, "Do you think Agent Joan Stevens can handle that?"

"Sounds doable to me" Joan answered. "I'll report back Tuesday."

It was raining Monday morning. Joan buckled herself into her only raincoat, a regulation spy-type trench coat. With a big smile, and a thumbs up to her mirror, she went out the door. It really felt like the beginning of an exciting new life. As she drove across town she considered what her alias would be. It would be embarrassing if she didn't recognize her "name." She decided on Janet Browner, as her sister, Janet, lived in another state.

Joan pulled up in front of Mrs. Shiffer's modest, modular home. She hurried up the path through an array of unrelated plants in old clay pots. At the front door she took a deep breath, then, with a mental *here we go* she pushed the doorbell and waited.

The door swung open and a grand-motherly Mrs. Shiffer stood in there smiling at Joan. Without questioning who Joan was, or even why she was there, she took Joan by the hand, welcoming her into her cozy living room.

"Your're all wet," Mrs. Shiffer exclaimed. "Sit over by the fire and I'll make you a cup of tea."

I'm Janet Browner," Joan began as she pulled off her soggy coat.

"I'm helping the county do a survey of local retirement homes. I wonder if I might ask you a few questions."

"Sure," Mrs. Shiffer agreed, "I might be able to help you, my sister owns a retirement home here in town."

They chatted for about an hour over tea and homemade cookies. Mrs. Shiffer was clearly glad to have the company, she answered questions and even volunteered further information. Joan busily wrote in her notebook. She was astonished how easy it had been.

Finally, with warm good-byes, Joan headed home.

That night she typed up her report. She wondered how much of her information Pete would actually find useful. She decided to give it all to him. He could decide for himself what he wanted to use.

Tuesday morning Joan was back at the Sure Help Agency. This time she walked right in. Pete was there behind his desk, almost as if he hadn't moved since her last visit. Joan triumphantly handed over her report. sat down, and waited as Pete thumbed through the papers. Finally, with a surprised smile, he looked up at Joan.

"Not bad" he allowed.

Sitting up, he addressed her with visibly heightened interest.

"You've got a lot of good stuff in here. How'd you do it?'

Joan described her strategy, who'd she'd been, how she'd gone about the questioning. Pete watched her, nodding every so often. When she finished he sat back.

"Well done," he said finally. "Want another assignment?"

Joan found it hard not to jump up and down. She was thrilled by her success.

"Sure" she replied eagerly, "What next?"

"I've got a divorce case here". He reached for another folder. "The husband hired me to watch his wife. He's not eager to pay spousal support and would like to catch her at some sort of indiscretion. It would involve sitting and watching, speaking to neighbors, that sort of thing, want it?"

Joan hesitated, somehow this wasn't the type of case she'd envisioned. Still high from her initial success, she accepted the assignment.

This time Pete gave her the folder to look through. "I need whatever you can get by Friday."

Joan consciously tried to put her initial concern out of her mind. She was looking forward to meeting her friend Bonnie at the Fishermen's Grill for lunch. Eager to share the news of her new job with Bonnie, she wanted to preserve every bit of her original excitement.

Joan arrived first. She settled into the snug Naugahyde booth and ordered coffee. Ten minutes later Bonnie still hadn't appeared. Joan pulled out the new folder from Pete. She felt the warm glow of professional pride as she spread it out in front of her. Smiling she began to familiarize herself with the case.

"God, this lady could have been me," she thought.

Bonnie arrived in a tornado of tense, angry, energy. Normally Bonnie was a totally confident, in-charge woman. Her Norwegian good looks were always beautifully groomed, her clothing polished and well cared for. Today she looked almost unfamiliar. Her randomly selected clothes weren't ironed. Her hair and make-up had recieved minimal attention.

Her friend glanced distractedly at Joan, then threw her coat and purse into the corner of the booth, and plunked down gracelessly. For a moment she stared determinedly out the window, then broke into a torrent of tears.

Joan reached across the table, "My God Bonnie, what's wrong."

With an effort Bonnie finally calmed herself enough to speak.

"Well, tell me how you're doing Joan, because I am right behind you. Bill's leaving."

There was another re-grouping moment, "He told me he just didn't want to be married anymore! The bastard! I had no idea. He's hired a private investigator to find something to pin on me so he can dance off without feeling bad. How tacky! How unfair!"

Bonnie sank back into tears.

Joan's discomfort swept away all desire to share her own happy news, "Private Investigator" suddenly sounded like dirty words she'd rather not speak out loud. To her relief the lunch conversation centered on Bonnie's situation. Listening was really all that was required of her.

Finally, Joan excused herself, anxious to get away. As they were finishing their coffee she gathered her things to leave. She held Bonnie's hand across the table again and answered Bonnie's original question.

"I'm doing okay now," she said. "Things are looking up. I know it's unbearable now, but it *will* get better." She gave Bonnie a hug and left in a rush of relief.

Joan tried to sort out her feelings as she sat motionless in her car. She sure didn't want to give up a career that seemed, in other ways, so promising.

"Darn it" she agonized, "I really thought I was going to enjoy this job. I know I'd be good at it, but I don't want to be a part of people's vindictive, manipulative divorces. To Pete it's just a job. To me it's assisting people in a sneaky game of one-upmanship. I want a job that helps people who really need it."

Suddenly a new, unfamiliar, thought swept her frustration away.

"Hey," she said out loud to the rear-view mirror. "I'm not completely helpless here. It doesn't have to be all or nothing!"

Joan started the car without a second thought and headed back to the Sure Help Agency. At the office door she hesitated. Inside she could hear a man's voice talking to Pete. Listening to the conversation she knew it was the man from the folder in her purse.

"We're going to court next Monday," the man finished, 'I need all you can give me by then. There must be something you can find."

"We'll do what we can," Pete answered noncommittally. "I have a new assistant working on it. I'll let you know."

There were good-byes, then a cocky looking man walked out the door. He stopped and looked at Joan, blatantly assessing every inch of her body. "Hi sweetheart," he said with a confident leer. Then he strode off down the hall.

Joan couldn't get inside fast enough. She slammed the door behind her and glared at Pete.

"I can't do this assignment. It's too close to home. The wife could be any one of a number of my friends. And that guy is a complete jerk!"

She began to calm down as it all spilled out.

"I'm sorry Pete, I just can't do it."

To her astonishment Pete didn't miss a beat.

"I knew you weren't going to do it. Too bad, I thought you had some talent. But this work isn't for people who want to pick and choose. I take the work I can get. I'm not a marriage counselor." Joan couldn't tell if he was disgusted or testing her. They sat there studying each other in a lengthy stalemate.

Finally, with a calmness and clarity that surprised her, Joan spoke, "Look Pete, I want to go on working with you. There must be investigative work that *helps* people. That's what I want. I'll finish this assignment, but I sure hope I never bump into that sleazy, conceited man again. You can train me Pete, and I could go out and drum up other business for the office. I know I could be useful. Would you be willing to do that?"

Pete gazed at her, lost in thought. They sat, silent again for several minutes and this time it unaccountably felt familiar and comfortable. Then Pete leaned forward and grinned at her. "Hey, I kind of like you working here. Adds a bit of surprise and humor to the office."

Then, in a more serious voice he continued.

"I'll tell you what. I've been asked to help the local police with missing children cases. Too many run-away kids. They all are heading for Sandy Cove these days. Seems it's a currently cool destination. If I work with you for a while to get you up to speed would that work suit you?"

"Yes, it really would, exactly!" Joan felt her original excitement flooding back. "Thanks so much Pete for understanding."

During the next few months Joan worked with Pete during the day. At night she studied books he gave her to take home. Pete was detailed, demanding, and thoughtful in his training and she loved the work. She liked feeling that she was helping parents and children, and she knew she was quickly becoming really good at what she was doing. The time flew by in a happy cloud of enthusiasm and hard work.

Six months later Joan leased the office next door to Pete's and a door was installed between the two offices.

As she proudly moved into her private office, Pete hung a new sigh in the hall between the two doors.

Swanson & Stevens

Private Investigators.

Drifting off to sleep that night, exhausted and happy, the thought of her grandmother's horoscope floated through Joan's mind. With effort she opened her eyes and looked out at the bright stars.

"Thanks Granny!" Then she smiled, hugged her pillow as if it were her wonderful new life, and fell asleep.

The Magnolia Tree

S ometime ago a seed, then hardy roots.

Slowly limbs, stretched out welcoming lovely flowers.

A lucky tree, nourished by its happy environment.

We've loved our tree, we've come to think of it as ours forever, yet, like ourselves, it has had its time of beauty and purpose.

It's ready to gracefully say goodbye. Grieving we wonder what can possibly fill the enormous gaping void?

The sun shines, the rain falls, in time, inevitably, new little sprouts peak out.

New beauty and inspiration needs room to flourish. In time we will bask in the newness.

Once Upon a Time 1

♥

There was a time when we were young when adventure trumped "should" and "ought to."

We'd climb out the window at night just to prove we could be bad. Scrambling back in we were giggling, thrilled, by our nervy naughtiness.

As times changed new windows opened. A new gift of freedom was in the air. With baby steps a "yes," then blowing in the wind, became an irresistible raging fire with a life of its own.

A new sense of self, a joy that sparkled with bright embers. Rising from the embers I learned to live on my own. No happy ever after, just a heap of empty ashes.

Once Upon A Time 2

A worn-out marriage,

Children fledging, flying.

Out of the blue love picks me up

In a whirl of new and now.

The gate's flown open,

two caught up in what feels like forever.

Time goes by. A friendship holds on.

The sound of a voice, news of our lives, suddenly

I'm told "no more."

My head understands, My heart can't let it go.

Alone, alone, alone.

Once Upon A Time 3

♥

Once upon a time the two of us went our own ways bringing home our interests, ideas, and projects. There were always stories to be shared, plans to be made, travel and adventures to be plotted. We were happy just as we were.

Once upon a time, there were hugs and kisses, loving and encouragement. Tom was my best friend and Barney's idol. For thirty-three years it didn't occur to me that one of us would ever be alone, and oh, certainly not so soon.

Once upon a time I came home
to find Tom sitting on the side
of the bed, desperately trying to
breathe.

One week later he was gone.

There isn't a Happy Ever After to
this tale.

An indifferent ogre just stepped
in and ended the story.

WARNING - BEWARE OF FAIRY STORIES

The Monopoly Game

We want to think that if we work hard enough, craft plans and schedules, and ready ourselves by holding on tight enough, we will be in perfect control, safe and happy.

Like a monopoly game we strategize, full of confident know-how and cunning, when suddenly the game changes.

The table has been dumped by someone in a huff.

What now? Even a "GO TO JAIL" card won't save us.

Here we are at Vista, sitting in our rooms, muddling along, trying to understand a world we could never have imagined.

At a distance we shout "Good Morning" through our masks and hope our eyes will communicate friendship.

Days go by, carts deliver endless entertainments to play with... alone.

Meals are delivered in plastic bags. "Heaven, there's chocolate ice cream to slowly savor. Trips to the scales indicate possibly cutting back a bit may be a good idea... someday... later.

Barney is a major source of entertainment and wisdom. He trots around the grounds checking the wildflowers, feeling the sun, looking for signs of new life . . . and maybe a cat. He doesn't make plans beyond his everyday needs. Change will happen to our specification - or not. Sadness and grief will be felt and dealt with. Babies will still arrive, and we, the old dogs, will learn new tricks and carry on.

Nothing is really new, change takes us forward, and here we go again, trying to be in control of "The New Normal." It's been so forever throughout centuries of change. We're just blowing in the wind, waiting for the next event. We are more, and less, than we think we are. Hope, love, laughter, and joy, hands held, hugs welcomed, tears heard and understood. There must be better ways to gently control the ups and downs of our lives. At the very least we can openly try. Putting away our egos we can find purpose in just life itself.

Navigating COVID

Brain Fog

H ow can this be!! My brain was iffy before, then Covid marched in claiming what's left. The fog creeps into everything. While playing its new game, it leaves the gate wide open. Precious wisdom and every day words have escaped, leaving me in an embarrassing quandary. Conversation has become a daunting new song and dance. I try to chat while I search

for the particular word I want. Bemused listeners try to be helpful. I add grumpy to the stressful search. There's a world of frustration

as we stand there playing a pitiful version of sign

language or the old game of twenty questions.

Brain Fog has propelled me backwards. I feel

like a young child, only to be seen and not heard.

Is this to be the new normal? Will it ever leave?

Navigating COVID

Dear Journal

I mportant Information to report lest we ever forget.

THE VIRUS. Another day, why? I did it all yesterday! I struggle up to shuffle in to make tea and toast, watch two depressing CNN hours.

Barney wanders in when he decides to get up. Outside a lusty sun smiles encouragingly. I finally respond. Dressed in any old thing (who cares), my mask is my new accessory. Barney and I are ready to walk.

Opened the door - oops, it's COLD! Back in for several more layers.

Barney looks bewildered.

Outside we come upon a parade of residents snaking along holding a long yellow plastic tape carefully marked at six-foot intervals. It looks like a long happy Chinese dragon. everyone cheerful and healthy. Barney and I scurry on. Doctor needs to see me, digitally, at ten o'clock. I have an annoying rash all over my chest. The site is not user friendly enough for me. Oh well.

11:00, my lunch comes to the door in a paper bag. Darn, what was I thinking when I checked the menu? Future orders will have chocolate ice cream. And wine. Oh well, wanting to hear a human voice, I dine with CNN - again.

Tidied up and napped. Waked to Barney eyes requesting a walk. Time for his security check of the premises. Heavy winds literally blow us along with the scurrying leaves. We went all the way around the outer perimeter. Whew! All's well. I turn the heater way up and work on some serious crosswords. Another meal arrives. This time I dine with PBS and one of Huell Howser's California Adventures. We bundle up for the day's last Barney outing - a quick, no nonsense rush around.

At home again there's face washing, hair brushing and tooth brushing, face moisturizing, pills and clock winding . . . then finally into our cozy bed to read until we drift off to Nod. Outside the wind blows the world around. Barney and I are safe and snug. We are so lucky to be where we are. Thank you universe, we'll check in with you in the morning.

Further reporting is not necessary, just read the above over, and over, and over... again.

GRUMPY

Light years ago, when we needed to vanquish COVID,

I cheerfully stepped forward and said "Okay, I can do this."

Yet here we are, stuck in the this and that of day after day,

same, same, same. Even my dog Barney is tired of it. We're tired of it all.

We've run out of cheerful.

We're feeling grumpy

Will it ever be over? How long can COVID hold us captive? We wait and wait as the world seems to be falling apart! Ever new problems pop up daily. It's way beyond what we ever could have dreamed of. Enough already!

I'm

tired

and

seriously

grumpy

It's time we fight back, together we can do this! (the current chant) Will we ever be able to fix it all? We look like prisoners, face masked, bleary eyed, hair ragged, desperately waiting for a new sense of fun and purpose.

I

suggest

a

new

activity

that

could

re-set

us

all

On a given night we'll all race outside. With great abandon we'll join in grumpy dances, arms and legs flailing about wildly (six feet apart of course) and singing grumpy songs with gusto. We will give each other virtual hugs until we drop to the grass looking at the stars and amusing the moon.

Finally, we'll return to our rooms able to repeat, once again, "Okay I can do this."

Repeat as required.

Dogs

An Ode to Peggy, Queen of The Universe

We thought the final new-home-move-in negotiations had been dealt with. Not so. When Tom drove up with the first load of packed boxes, a final meeting was clearly indicated. Peggy, a smallish, border collie-like dog, clearly the official Neighborhood Watch, met Tom with authoritative barks. She was there to interview the new owners. Luckily Tom managed the interview appropriately. We were allowed to move in.

Peggy, it turned out, was a border collie/corgi mix. She looked like a small border collie, black and white with tasteful patches of tan. On the other hand, she had short corgi legs and paws that turned out in a graceful ballet first position like a corgi. With great aplomb she made her style the perfect dog design. She carried herself with authority and grace. Though she'd been a foundling puppy, there was no doubt, ever, that she was in charge.

Busy settling in we didn't see Peggy for a while. Then, one evening as we sat on the back porch with our first dinner guests, she appeared at the bottom of the steps. I noticed her but paid no particular attention. As time passed it became impossible *not* to notice her. She sat there looking up at us with intense, sincere, interest. Finally, she was invited up. She trotted up the steps as if she was just a little late for the party and gracefully accepted a few tasty scraps.

It was the beginning of a long and loving friendship. I often felt that I'd known Peggy in some other lifetime. She started to come down for a visit every day. Some cynics might suggest it was for the endless treats that were issued, but I knew she was there for a pleasant day's visit. I "trained" her to sit with a treat on her nose until I said "OK," and to roll over. None of it was a challenge. Sitting up was a constant part of her repertoire. She did it all with ease and style. Her favorite job was herding anything that moved. One day Tom found her gently guiding a mole across the driveway.

My women's group was at the house one evening. We always ended the evening by holding hands in a circle. To our surprise, Peggy was right in place, sitting up, waiting to join the circle. We held paws as we said goodnight.

Our neighbors generously allowed the love affair to flourish. We had a happy grandchild-like relationship, all the fun and none of the responsibility. What could be more wonderful? Her furry presence became a symbol of the coziness and warmth of our home. She arrived first thing in the morning. She'd announce herself with a sharp bark, and wait for Tom to rush down and let her in. She'd trot straight upstairs for a short nap on the fluffy flotaki rug. Often, she'd be covered with little redwood cones and twigs that she'd collected on the way down. We jokingly talked of marketing "The Peggy Forest Accessory Collection," or, after a beach outing, "The Peggy Seaside Collection."

We celebrated Peggy's 18th birthday with her family. There was a special cake and various small gifts. Shortly after the party she suffered a couple of small strokes. She'd have moments of thoughtfully staring into space in a peaceful confusion. Often, she had a difficult time walking a straight line, constantly veering off to the right. Tom commented that he she needed her steering realigned. She had days of bouncing down in the morning like a puppy, the next day she'd get confused and we'd find her going around in circles. At night we no longer just let her out to go home, we, or her owner, would carry her.

She still knew when it was time for me to make dinner. She'd let me know with a gentle nudge. If I didn't appear to pay attention she'd carry on with little sharp barks until I'd attend to dinner. Though she'd become quite deaf, a little blind, and seemingly in a deep sleep she still knew when we were sitting down for tea or dinner.

It was clear that it was the end of the road. We knew we'd been saying goodbye for some time. Finally, she wasn't even able to lie down. For the first time she seemed truly uncomfortable. She just stood there with her nose on the floor. We said a final goodbye as we left her that night. The next day she went to her vet who helped her on her way to a happier place. Our neighbor assured us she'd moved on to be crowned Queen of The Universe. It was the obvious destiny for "our" Peggy. It felt good to know she was on duty there, but we, and our home, was never same without her.

Dogs

♥

My Pal Barney

We were busy moving into our wonderful new home, arranging furniture, hanging pictures, putting boxes of books back on their shelves. Finally, we felt settled, and yet . . . something, was missing. We realized we needed a dog. My husband, Tom, grew up in Scotland. On our numerous trips to Scotland we'd fallen in love with West Highland terriers. With a rush of excitement, I rushed to my computer to find a Westie rescue site. Having found one I had a short conversation with a woman who said we would need to fill out a form for them to make sure we would be suitable owners.

After a short conversation with their office I was told that we would need to fill out a form to ensure them we'd be suitable owners. The form arrived. It was rather like trying to get into college. They needed exact measurements of our outside area, recommendations from friends, descriptions of activities that would include a dog, and how much we felt it would cost to care for a Westie (boy, did I underestimate that one!) I carefully filled it all out and sent it off. We received an email saying they currently had no Westies!

"Well heck" I grumped to Tom. "let's forget it for now. When the right dog comes along we'll know it."

One week later, on a Sunday morning, we were sitting in bed, enjoying our tea and toast, Tom reading the paper, I busy with the crossword and the funnies. Suddenly the phone rang. It was my friend Nancy in Santa Cruz.

"Look at the dog rescue section of the paper" she said with great excitement. "There's a picture of your dog. You'd better get down to the shelter fast." Sure enough, the picture of Barnaby got us up, dressed, and on our way. The ad read "Only the best for Barnaby, followed by a long list of glowing traits: "Barnaby is a beautiful dog with a handsome face, luxuriously soft hair and a small but solid build. He has an A+ personality." His picture clearly said "come on, I'm waiting for you." They told us he was part poodle and part west highland terrier,

SIDE NOTE: Several years later, I was given a DNA test for Christmas. It said he was 75% poodle, 11.5% other terrier, and, the big surprise, 11.5% Pekinese! Clearly the perfect mixture.

At the shelter Barnaby was just returning from a walk. The volunteer picked him up and put him into Tom's arms. No question about it, It was love at first sight.

We were told that he had been kept in a crate, day and night, in a hot San Joaquin valley garage and punished if he soiled his crate. When he was rescued he had been sent to the Santa Cruz shelter where it had taken three months to get him well enough to be adoptable. We knew Barnaby would have a happy, comfortable home with us. As we left the shelter our first decision was to change his name to Barney. Tom suggested that he could save "Barnaby" for when he needed to sign checks.

On our way home, we stopped at a pet store to pick up necessities; a kennel, a comfortable bed, toys, a leash and collar with ID tag, a brush and some starter food. The shelter volunteer had suggested that when we got home Tom should take Barney for walk through each room, allowing plenty of time for Barney to investigate everything of interest. He carefully checked it all out and gave it a dog version of a "thumbs up." It was sad to find that when we called him he'd approach us with his head down, as if expecting to be punished. It took him a quite a while to realize that he didn't have to be endlessly anxious.

All went well until bed time. I put a nice towel in his kennel and settled him in the den next door to our bed room. The moment I left the room heart rending yips stopped me in my tracks. Not sure of how to proceed I called my daughter. "Just put the kennel at the end of your bed." she advised. That took care of the problem.

The next morning, I took him for a walk to introduce him to our neighbors. One of my friends asked if he was trained. I had no idea. I looked at Barney and said "sit." Barney sat. I was astonished. Later in the day I took him to a park for a walk. He was beside himself. It was like he'd never seen grass before. He ran and ran in wild circles, rolled endlessly on the grass, clearly smiling as he checked each new wonder. Every so often, in the midst of all the fun, he'd stop to make sure that I was still there.

Barney had serious separation issues. When we left him in the house alone he shredded the door jamb with his claws, or opened cupboards to spread garbage around. We bought a metal corral that we put in the living room for when we went out. Barney managed to move the whole corral around the living room. Wondering how he did it, Tom secretly watched to see how Barney managed to push it around. It turned out that he would back up, then run at the other side and leap at the bars with his paws moving the whole thing along. In so many ways over the years Barney has endlessly demonstrated how clever he is. When he really wants to do something, he manages to find a way to do it.

The three of us settled in and, in no time, life with Barney became an endless, easy-going, joy. Barney and Tom were fast friends, playing and working together. when it was time for a sit-down Barney was curled up next to Tom. I was appreciated mainly for meals.

We had many good years together. Barney traveled with us, long trips and short. He had a dog seat in the back seat that allowed him to gaze out the window when we were on the road. When we dined at an outside restaurant he would politely sit under the table entertaining himself by chewing through his leash. All said, the pleasure and fun Barney gave us way outshined the occasional naughtiness.

Then the dreadful time came when our Tom died. Barney and I grieved together. We tried to feel whole but it was hard. Everything was different. I was busy trying to get on top of all that needed to be done. Barney didn't have his pal to play with ... I was just plain boring. His insecurity returned. If I was anywhere in the Park without him he'd cleverly find a way to get out and try to find me. He became known as Houdini. Nice neighbors were constantly arriving at my door with Barney in their arms.

Time went by and, finally, I decided to make a major move to Santa Barbara. It was difficult letting go of our lives up North. Everything in our new world was new. Once again Barney's separation issues reappeared.

There were upsetting dog rules that neither of us enjoyed. We had a trainer come to suggest ways I could leave Barney when I needed to leave him. The trainer said the answer was to put him in his crate when I left, saying that he would get used to it. She assured me that he would learn to feel comfortable and safe there. Neither Barney nor I felt that would work. He had, after all, been there done that. I promised him I wouldn't do that. His happiness was all I cared about. If he couldn't come with me I'd stay in the room with him.

It didn't take long however for Barney to charm most everyone. When we were out for walks residents greeted us with a happy "Hello Barney," often they ask to pet him. Barney graciously allow the strokes, it's a win-win for all. He's Mr. Congeniality, trotting along like a CEO, inspecting the campus each morning, visiting with friends, entertaining always, and caring for those who wish they had a dog of their own. He's even found a lovely girlfriend, Pepper, a classy black poodle. Best of all he is my constant best friend.

Dogs

Stress Relief

You are on your way home from work, you're mentally making lists of what is waiting for you when you get home and you are already late. To make things worse the traffic is hopelessly stalled. It's time for some stress relief. I'd like to share with you what I've learned from observing dogs in cars.

First of all dogs live in the moment. Unlike humans they aren't stressed by (except when there is possibility that it hears the word "Vet") circumstances you are feeling. Every trip is an exciting adventure, or at the very least a pleasurable, private time spent with a best friend. Very few dogs appear to be concerned about driving conditions, or are worried about getting to a destination "on time." Each dog has its own style, finding amusements to pass the time happily. Watching dogs in cars can be a very relaxing, not to mention fun, activity.

The following are scenarios you might recognize;

Suddenly, in the car ahead, something small and furry leaps gleefully from the front seat to the back. It's **Excited Dog** in action. The fluff ball rushes back and forth in the back seat, then, a split second later, it disappears and pops up in the rear window again looking like it is practicing on a trampoline. Finally, the two button eyes, black nose, and pink tongue are wistfully smiling at me. It's tempting to wave, but the small, busy, beast is off to start all over again.

As we all know, a dog hurling itself around in a car can be dangerous. A friend told me of one dog's solution. A preschool mother had just dropped off her child at school. She was heading home with their standard poodle in the car. As she drove off she became aware that people in other cars were pointing and laughing at something in the back seat. At the next stop light she turned to the back seat to see what was going on. The poodle had comfortably settled itself in the old-style baby car seat. It was sitting up with legs straight through the correct holes in the fabric, paws resting on the front tray. He was looking quite pleased with himself. It became the dog's favorite way to ride whenever the car seat was free.

Another dog passenger style is **The Interviewer**. This activity is best practiced in slow traffic, usually done from the back of an open truck bed. The dog rushes back and forth, from side to side, looking for another dog to talk to. With loud barks and yaps, tails wagging, they yell at each other.

"Hey over there where are you off to?

What kind of work do you and that guy do?

It's kind of boring back here, seen anything interesting?

It's tricky for the interviewer since a disrespectful comment, or growling sneer can be regretted if both trucks stop at the same place. Perhaps there is an *"I was just kidding"* kind of bark for such tricky moments.

One time when I was visiting my sister she asked me if I'd go to the hardware store for her. She suggested that her dog Bunty, a large Border Collie, would like to go with me. She gave me Bunty's doggles, (glasses that would keep her eyes safe when she had an opportunity to enjoy an open window). Bunty didn't seem to mind wearing them at all. It was blissfully-heads-out all the way until we turned into the parking lot where there was a truck with a couple of dogs in the back. They started making unpleasant comments at Bunty. She couldn't get the doggles off fast enough.

Then there is **The Nose**, another familiar sight. Tensed and focused, eyes squinting, nose twitching, ears flowing or flapping in the wind. It's doing its best to unravel the lavish sensory over-load outside. Some poor noses aren't given access to a truly adequate window opening. Wet nose, painfully squeezed out the quarter inch of open window, mouth dribbling down the window glass, they steadfastly do their best with what they have to work with,

One of my favorites is the **Solemn, Sincere**, front seat passenger. I was following one the other day. I had noticed the two handsome ears sticking up over the right seat head-rest. There was no funny business going on. Every so often a good-looking shepherd snout would turn to the left, seemingly to discuss what he'd seen with the driver. Then eyes straight forward again and no more movement. I decided that he'd quietly lost himself into his private dog musings.

Another version of the front seat companion is **The Lover**. This dog can't contain its head-over-heels love for his owner. It just can't do enough to show its total devotion. The Lover needs a bench seat in the front. It starts rather like Good Dog. From behind, you notice a slight but obvious inclining of the body to the left. Then the body slowly begins to sidle ever closer and closer to the driver. Inevitably there are stolen kisses and ear licks Often the dreamy head rests its head on a shoulder. If there are no reciprocal pats or strokes there are subtle reminders of its presence; a gentle poke of the nose, a paw laid gently on the driver's leg, or a long sincere stare.

In closing, I'll share a funny true story. A friend and I were having lunch at a lovely restaurant near the beach. We were seated at the window, looking out at the beautiful day outside. Suddenly a snappy green Jaguar sports car, top down, zipped into a parking space right outside where we were sitting. There was a handsome man, and in the other seat, a girl with lavish red hair. I started to grump to my friend, "Why do men of a certain age seem to require such obvious "accessories?" When we looked out again the man was going around the car to open the door for the redhead. A gorgeous beautifully groomed red setter leapt out.

We had a good laugh. We decided that the man was not only handsome, he was smart enough to have chosen such a perfect companion.

Gambay's Extra Extra

♥

Options and Choices

My daughter Barbie, granddaughter Margot and I were planning a trip to Sweden. As we were packing we suddenly found that we had a free luggage allowance. "Well heck, why not take everything we might possibly need." BIG MISTAKE! We found ourselves endlessly struggling with our absurdly huge suitcases. To make it harder, Scandinavia welcomed us with an unexpected full-on heat wave.

After a wonderful stay with relatives in a beautiful rural area of southern Sweden we were off to Stockholm. We had managed to drag our behemoths several blocks to the train stop, Barbie settled herself gratefully on the only blistering hot bench, Margot, a ballerina, stood there in high heels looking gorgeous and unperturbed. I, as always, was busily rummaging around in my oversized bag; this time looking for pen. "I've lost my pen" I wailed with frustrated scowl . . . a few seconds later... a grumpy "that's the story of my life!' With a big smile Margot looked over, "That sounds like a good name for a book." It would be a book about the outcome of the choices we make.

It's worth pondering a bit about the losses in our lives. Most of us lose things all the time; from small, insignificant things, to the deeply painful losses of loved ones. Every loss has own intensity and scope. When the loss is new and simply too painful, it's hard to see a possible up-side to the loss. As time goes by we find ourselves making new choices, finding new opportunities, asking ourselves, "what do I want to do or try, now? " From the distance of time we can see clearly how much we've grown since the initial experience of the loss.

My silly pen frustration faded away. The train arrived. I chose to forget pens, and writing. I settled in to enjoy my day. We were zipping along gazing out at the beautiful countryside. I'd completely forgotten the pen.

Every day is filled with options and decisions to be made. Every moment requires a decision. Will I do this or that. For example, If I let go of a habit - for instance "I don't want to keep eating food that is really bad for me." This is when we need to stop and ask yourself "what options do I have to make a difference now? how will I deal with the loss of that habit." What will we choose to replace it with that changes us. We become a different person. Happily, decisions aren't necessarily forever. As long as we take responsibility for our choices, new options are possible.

The same things are true of the big changes we are facing as our world seems to be changing every day. In some ways it feels downright scary, but at the same time it is a time that we can we can hopefully opt to work together as we find new ways to heal our planet, new ways to to treat each other with compassion, new creative, innovative, ways to solve our many problems.

Over endless centuries there have been a multitude of decisions made. How many have been positive choices and how many have been total disasters? We are living in a time that has become more and more difficult to cope with. The decisions we make now will decide what we leave for our children. It can't be about "me," it has to be about our entire world.

Gambay's Extra Extra

Beach Walking

It's the perfect day for a trip to the beach. I call my friend Nancy to see if she and her dog Henry would like to join Barney and me. Great excitement on all sides. The excitement revs up in the back seat as the dogs smell the ocean way before we get there. We find a parking spot and the two anxious dogs leap out heading for the beach, dragging us across the parking lot to the sand where we can let them off leash. Off they go, running in circles of pure joy. Other dogs join in fun after appropriate dog introductions are negotiated. Every bit of flotsam and jetsam is examined and decisions are made as to whether or not a pee is required. We watch carefully to make sure that they don't invite themselves to the nicely laid out picnics.

We reach the water line and settle into a comfortable pace. After a while we find a big log to sit on. We watch the long lines of pelicans gracefully gliding barely above the water. There are happy small children with their buckets and shovels, the older ones are building drift wood hide outs. The dogs rest by our legs.

Nancy and I have known each other for ages. We met at work a long time ago. We started chatting, and over the years, since we've chatted our way through all our ups and downs. Beach walking is a perfect place to dive into current concerns.

This particular day I was feeling particularly glum. It had been four years since my husband had died. I was tired of living alone. I wanted to meet someone, that is to say, a man, to enjoy my life with. Nancy had been comfortably on her own for years. "It doesn't have to be a man" she said. "You can enjoy yourself with your women friends." "So true" I thought yet being with a man is a whole different world - if it's the right man. I started home mulling over our conversation.

On my way home, I stopped by the market to find something for dinner. The market had snappy *little* carts, rather like sports cart models. I was zipping along throwing things into the cart, a turkey sandwich, some lovely Fuji apples, a couple of small cartons of Three Sisters Ice cream (the very best ever!), a 6-pack of Angry Orchard Cider, and a large bar of dark chocolate (all the world knows that it's good for you). As I hurrying around a corner I literally bumped into another sports cart driven by a very good-looking man. We stood there laughing. It was tempting to blurt out, "Gosh, I'm not hurt, but it might be best if we sat down for a cup of coffee, or maybe dinner, or for ever after.

Oh well, dream on. I decided it was time to be a bit more proactive. Some friends had good e-dating experiences. They urged me to give it a go. My first coffee date was with a dear little elderly man, a former engineer that had lost his wife. We chatted about this and that and decided we'd meet again. At our second meeting I sat there struggling how to say, "Sorry, this just isn't working for me." We'd met twice and hadn't laughed once. A good sense of humor is high on my Prince Charming list.

My next e-date was more hopeful. He was pleasant looking, had lots to say, and was astonishingly out front about his interest in sex, nothing nuanced or subtle about it. We dated for some time and had some very good times, but I finally realized that 1) he was really only interested in his family, not interested in my family at all; 2) he was very Christian and wanted me to be — that didn't work for me; and finally 3) he was a total Republican - I'm very not!

So much for e-dating. At 85 there aren't many options left. Yet it's still painful to see elderly couples walking along holding hands, choosing things at the market, or enjoying a good laugh together, or just helping each other.

I live in Santa Barbara now. Before the evil COVID lock down Barney and I would go down to the beach. as before, he would smell the beach before we got there and the excitement grew. We'd rush across the parking lot and down the stairs to the beach. I'd undo his leash and off he'd go. Sadly, it was the rare dog willing to play with him with despite his best overtures. It's not easy to slowly collect new friends We miss you Nancy and Henry.

Mother Nature

♥

It's not easy to be a mother! We do our best to deal with Baby's needs until, in time, a balance shifts. Our resources wane. It's time for Baby to launch. Time for mother to embrace a new life. **Mother Nature watches it all.**

From ants to elephants we all follow the same predictable arc; birth, life, death. Earth itself has it's limits, we seem to feel that it's all about us. We chose to forget the needs of other living thing things. **Mother Nature watches it all.**

The balance has shifted, we still want to think we humans deserve it all, can take it all, can control it all. As our easy lives get harder, problems are harder to solve. We're scared, we turn on each other.

As our precious planet struggles to make its way.

Mother Nature watches it all.

Mother Nature seems to have had enough. She Rains

floods of tears, shakes our world with angry quakes

and tornadoes, erases fields and homes with fire

and flood as we hopefully rebuild, over and over

again. We wonder, what next? Are we too late?

Mother Nature watches it all.

Our big brains feel they have an answer. We can

simply take over Mars. Would we go? Most of us
wouldn't be needed, but who would be guiding the
robots? Plan B?

We could simply leave like helpless dinosaurs?

Mother Earth has given up, she's just plain tired.

The Great Gift Migration

♥

I moved not so long ago, an agony of
choices, what to take, how can I leave that?
I emptied my home, watching treasures
walk out the door with family and friends.
I tried to gift special pals with items I
I thought they'd enjoy. Then I packed up
and left with way many too many boxes.
I landed in my new, very small space, still
trying to find happy homes for every item.
If I thought something was perfect for a
friend I'd blatantly woo my target with

spiels of how they could use the item.

How many "thank you so much's" were

followed by quick trips to the next

regifting drawer to await its next move?

Keep in mind, I'm a Great Depression era

baby. Throwing things out, half used

pencils, old wooden boxes with snappy

advertising, telephones no longer used.

Then there were the linens, paper plates, and

entertainment items for parties I no longer

give. Yet I just can't help feeling that

someone, somewhere, would love to have them.

Today I received a sweet gift from a dear

friend who'd been clearing out her sister's house

back East. She'd come across two coasters with

pictures of handsome foxes on them. Knowing

I love animals she'd sent them to me.

The coasters have settled in with my many

other animal coasters. I imagine them all sharing

their travels from one regifting drawer to the next.

Thank you, my friend, for thinking of me. The foxes

will enjoy a rest, then travel on to the next drawer.

Ice Cream Social

We're invited to an ice Cream Social. Yay, What fun.

I sidle up to the colorful table to check the options.

I finally decide on cookie crunch in a crisp cone. Mmmmm, my first lick, a little jolt of icy, creamy,

flavor melts on my tongue. I slowly move it around in my mouth spreading the pleasure. Heaven! Holding the

cone I turn it slowly, keeping it tidy, . . . oops! It's

really starting to melt. Time to go for it with lovely,

satisfying, slurps. Oh dear, it's all gone. I dab around

my sticky mouth trying to look like an adult again.

It's tricky to eat an ice cream cone and be social at

the same time. Both activities require attention.

Luckily, it's not a problem! We slurp and laugh at

ourselves as we enjoy being our young selves again.

Life's Indignities

♥

For someone like my sister, a woman who'd been in charge of her life for years, it was hard for her to admit that she could no longer live her life in her usual efficient, cheerful, easy way. She'd suddenly found herself in the long slide of dealing with breast cancer. With her characteristic humor she announced that "Getting old is just one indignity after another."

Now, years later, I find myself dealing with the same kinds of situations and indignities, I am in relatively good shape, yet there are still plenty of day to day indignities and annoyances.

I stand at the mirror wondering why there seems to be so much extra skin, It has nowhere to go. It arranges itself in little wrinkles and unwanted lumps.

I walk out of CVS with an embarrassing cart full of panty liners, I want to say loudly, "These are for my ancient granny." When I get home I carefully cover it all with a beach towels as I take it to my room,

I start a conversation and suddenly find that brain fog has stepped in, and I've lost what I was wanting say.

I even find it annoying that there are so many people my age, and older, that seem to be in great shape. It turns out that some people grew up exercising and being athletic. In my family there was no interest in being athletic. We just did what was needed to be done and carried on. It wasn't in my genes to love running endlessly back and forth playing things like field hockey (sorry, just a grumpy surge.)

Back when I was teaching image classes one of the rules was to accent the things you liked about your bod, and cover the parts you didn't like. We were in Denmark some time ago, I wanted to find something to wear that was more appropriate for the heat wave we were experiencing. I found a nice little store and picked out a pair of cropped pants. They seemed to be exactly what I needed . . . except I was concerned about the state of my battered legs. When the sales lady came to ask if I liked the pants. I told her I was concerned about allowing my legs to be seen. "I don't know what to do" I whined. She looked rather surprised then, eye to eye, she announced "Just live with them!"

I've thought of her great advice so often. She'd given me a precious gift. I learned to live with what I'm lucky to have. What the heck, I *am* old, and have a world of good things in my life. I no longer try to be anything more,

113

or less, than I am. I'll think of my sister and laugh with her as life's endless indignities continue to pop up.

Curiosity Can Indeed Kill The Cat

♥

Let's face it, we live on a tiny planet in a vast universe of planets. Somewhere up there in the clouds there is a force that tends to them all. When a planet is old enough it graduates to being sent out into the galaxy.

This beautiful little planet, the one we live on, was finally old enough to graduate and take its place in the universe. After considerable discussion in the clouds it was given the name "Earth." It was time for Universal Planet Designers Inc. to step in. It was made clear that this very young, delicate, planet would need special plans. After numerous meetings the company came up with an appropriate mission statement. "We want Earth to be the finest, most lasting, of our many projects. "

The Fauna Department went to work. They started by testing tiny life forms. They found that their test organisms were flourishing. They handed the project on to the Life Style Analysts Department. Overly enthusiastic, they foolishly leapt ahead to design REALLY BIG life; cool, enormous, animals that they called pterodactyls and dinosaurs. In no time the company realized that they'd made a big mistake. The animals were way too much for such a small planet. They erased that idea and designed new, midsized animals, and sent them on to the art department. With wild abandon, and a large pallet of colors, and innovative design elements, they produced a world of beautiful, unique, and sometimes downright funny beings. Each group was equipped with the knowledge of how and where their particular species would live, and how they would thrive and pass their wisdom on to their children (they understood that in time, they would pass away). The Life Style Department made sure that each species could find and use the tools they would need to thrive.

The Life Style Universal Planet Designers Inc. was very pleased with itself. It had been a fun and successful, project. No one wanted it to see it end. One of the crew members suggested trying a new experiment. "Let's give one species a larger brain and see what a difference it would make. They gave the larger brains to the great apes and called them Human Beings.

Slowly humans learned how to live and work together, happily begetting plenty of replacements - and then some. As their groups grew they needed more space on the Planet and more and more food. Other animals had the same needs, but their smaller brains left them with fewer options. Meanwhile humans, with their larger brains, were finding more and more ways to take, and own, whatever they wanted . . . including other animals. Killing others has become easier and easier.

We seem to feel that Earth was designed just for us. Our curiosity is endless, we can do and have whatever we want, simply because our big brains can find ways for us to do so. Once upon a time a king would bravely ride out in front of his army. Now he can wipe out the entire planet with the push of a button.

So here we are, our big brains have left us with a host of serious problems: vast populations. a depleted planet, and now global warming and seemingly more and more forms of deadly viruses. If we can't bring ourselves to deal with all of the serious problems at hand, our big brains can't save us on our little planet.

If a new Design Team gives us another try, that is if there will still be a planet called Earth, I hope that they remember the lessons learned in their first attempt.

I Surprise Myself.

♥

Sitting at my computer, fiddling around, I randomly clicked on an unknown key. To my delight I suddenly had a never-ending loop of my considerable collection of photos. My life was right there, open to be enjoyed all over again. I found myself reaching out to touch and send hugs and kisses to each picture.

There are children playing in the garden, Tom putting up yet another, hopefully squirrel-proof, bird feeder, Barney romping, trips to the beach with friends, pictures of special parties and table settings. Then the many pictures of my beloved garden and endless pictures of Barney.

A wonderful Viking river boat trip, visits with far away friends and family. Then the other wonderful trips: Utah, Yellowstone, and to the Canadian Rockies.

Then of course the holidays, so many pictures of all of us playing and laughing.

I was asked one day if it didn't make me sad to look back at all that was, and is no more. My answer was "absolutely not!" The pictures endlessly remind me of the wonderful life I have lived (try it, it's an immediate upper.)

A final Note: any life has its ups and downs; there are moments of wild happiness, and times of deep sadness. There is progress, then stress and frustration. We can save ourselves by accepting that in the end... despite it all, IT'LL ALL WORK OUT.

One More Thing

I hope you enjoyed reading *It'll All Work Out,* and if you did, ***please*** leave a review. Reviews really help, and they can be as short as you want (longer too if so inclined). Since you're reading the print edition, just point your phone or tablet camera at the QR Code below that will take you straight to the appropriate *It'll All Work Out* review page...

Acknowledgments

My heartfelt thanks to the friends and family who have helped and encouraged me to put this book together. They include Vera Nelson, Joy Winer, Lyn Follett Julie Snyder, Roger Whalen, and Judy Garvens who gave me the final push.

Illustrations by Merrillee Ford

Special thanks to Tom and Alison for help with formatting and layout.

Made in the USA
Monee, IL
31 January 2023